End NailBiting Forever!

W. E. Smith
© 2022

The solution is in your
hands right now

You can be free
from this

Author: W.E. Smith

Project Manager: W.E. Smith

Publisher: Willhouse Publishing LLC

This book may be purchased for educational, business, or sales promotional use. For information kindly contact the Author.

Willhousepublishing@gmail.com

Book cover art purchased from iStock by Ghetty Images.

Trust the Process

Dedication

This book is dedicated to You the reader & to

every nail biter who believed they could never

stop this self destructive behavior.

Stay consistent

Acknowledgments

I want to thank all the people who purchased

my first book Healing Rainbows. The success

of that book encouraged me to write this book

and more to come. Thank You!

Free Yourself

Table of Contents

You Got this

PREFACE

I bit my fingernails for nearly half a century. I tried many different remedies and solutions in an effort to stop biting my nails but nothing seemed to work until I discovered a simple solution. I have never heard of it or read it in any books or articles but I promise you right here and now that the solution that will be introduced in this guide actually works. I implore you to not allow the simplicity of this solution to detour you from wholeheartedly trying it. It will work for you and your loved ones, family, or friends who suffer from this affliction. I have also learned some life lessons from this journey where this same solution was applied to other areas of my life which allowed me to have success in other areas of my life as well so I will share some of them with you in case they could possibly be a help to your life like they were to mine.

Now after years of receiving many nice compliments about my nails, sometimes nail-biting seems like nothing more than a distant memory. New friends that I have made in the last few years do not even believe that for the vast majority of my life, my fingers were bloody and scarred nubs. When I tell them they think I am exaggerating. It saddens me and my heart hurts for people who bite their nails, especially when I see children and teens with this horrible deforming habit. Seeing grown men with their fingers in their mouths bothers me as well because I know from memory how embarrassed those men are likely to feel about that habit and how helpless they feel in being able to stop doing it. But keep reading this book. I got you!

Nail-biting will not typically cause permanent damage. But it definitely has its downsides: It can make your nails grow weird. If you damage the tissue around your nails, they may stop growing the way they should. This can give you abnormal-looking fingernails. It can spoil your smile. You can chip, crack, or break your teeth when you bite your nails. Over time, nail biting can even cause jaw problems. Nail-biting can make you sick. Our hands are a hotbed for germs, and nails are the perfect hideout. When you're putting your fingers in your mouth multiple times a day, it increases your chances of getting sick. Plus, the skin damage you can cause when you bite your nails creates an easy way for germs to get in. But no worries. I am going to show you how to have attractive, aesthetically pleasing, and healthy nails for the rest of your life.

Please enjoy this little book and spread the word, so that we can End nail-biting Now!

I am congratulating you in advance for your success and freedom from nail-biting. it is yours today! Thank you for buying this booklet.

You are Outstanding

Chapter One

INTRODUCTION

I wrote this book a few years ago and it was a very short book, more like a small pamphlet where I just gave my stop nail-biting solution. I sold it for five dollars and it has helped many people but people would continually come back to me asking about my journey or my struggles. I realized that people valued my solution much more after they heard how I overcame decades of fingernail-biting. Especially after they learned that often my habit and the everyday state of my nails were worse than a lot of my readers. Allow me to start off by saying; If you are either not concerned or you simply feel you do not need to know my journey or the history of nail-biting, that is completely understandable, and you would prefer to rather get straight to the point or directly to the solution. In that case, I encourage you to go directly to chapter three of this book to learn my Stop Nail-Biting Forever Solution. Maybe after you have read it you might be interested in how I arrived at this solution. But if you want to read this book in the order I believe may give you the clearest perspective of my journey to nail-biting freedom. Then please continue with me.

Within the pages of this little book, there is a simple yet phenomenally effective solution that will show you how to End fingernail-biting forever. No gimmicks, no tricks, no creams or chemicals. Just a proven way of ending the horrible habit of nail-biting. There are simple everyday actions that will immediately change your nail-biting behavior. This book is short, sweet, and to the point. You can STOP Today!

I want you and everyone else to be free from this horrible habit. After finally having aesthetically pleasing hands and nails I was so excited about the nail growth that I let my nails get way too long because I could not bring myself to cut them. Honestly, I would constantly scratch myself or cut myself with my nails because they had been bloody nubs for my entire life and I was so unused to having not just long nails but any fingernails at all. I was never upset about scratching or cutting myself because it was simply a wonderful reminder that I finally had some fingernails. One day a girlfriend showed me how to file them in a fashion that removed any sharp edges and allowed me to keep my length. But eventually, because of my lifestyle and work, I had to shorten them to a more reasonable length. It feels wonderful to do things like point or hold things with my nails showing in full view. It feels great to scratch an itch without using a foreign object, to pick up things I could not normally pick up with my nubs, even though I had become quite efficient with my nubs from a lifetime of practice. With Great Joy, I can still remember the first time I could tap my nails on glass and make noise.

Men know this and possibly ladies as well but after a day of school or work wearing long socks, our ankles and calves can get very dry, and as soon as we remove the socks our legs immediately begin to itch. Honestly, I am a little embarrassed to admit the truth that I almost cried the first time I removed my socks and was able to scratch my own legs without having to use a foreign object to scratch my legs and ankles. I remember the first time I surprised my girlfriend by scratching her back for her when it was itching and the response of surprise and excitement, she had in my nail growth. Every nail-biter should experience these wonderfully natural things. You can experience everything I have just mentioned and more. You are holding your solution in your hands right now. it is all up to you!!

Chapter Two

<u>MY STORY</u>

Some nail-biters are occasional or moody biters, but then you have nail-biters like myself who seem to live their entire life with their fingers in their mouths. But no matter which level of nail-biter you are, I am willing to bet you want to stop NOW. I had been a nail-biter for over 45 years. It started when I was a very young child, and it never stopped. Because of nail-biting, my fingers were constantly bleeding and swelling. I would regularly be in pain from everyday situations such as the juice from an orange or even hot water touching my fingers while washing my hands or washing dishes. As a young boy, my nail biting did not really bother me. It was a family tradition, my mother as well as my little brother both bit their nails as well. It seemed completely normal but as I grew into my teens, the humiliation of this disfiguring habit began to Seriously haunt me.

Every picture taken of me during my time in middle school, high school, and until my early 30s clearly shows me hiding my fingers from the camera. Most of the pictures reveal me with my hands balled up into a fist to prevent my mangled nails from being seen. I remember being too embarrassed to eat with someone I admired or to hold hands with someone to whom I was attracted. I remember the many times my nails were seen and commented on, to my embarrassment. Over the years, I tried many different things to stop biting my nails. I tried punishments or penalties like painfully slapping my hand every time I caught myself biting my nails or doing pushups every time I placed my hands in my mouth, just to name a few. Family members and friends tried to help by suggesting remedies such as placing bad-tasting solutions on my nails, taping my fingernails up with scotch tape, and duct tape, or wearing gloves all day, but nothing seemed to work. If I achieved any nail growth, I would quickly destroy it all with just a few minutes of nail-biting.

One day in the bathroom of a restaurant a truth or revelation came alive to me as I watched people leaving the bathroom and I realized that most people do not wash their hands after they use the bathroom. In horror, it also occurred to me that most people do not wash their hands or use hand sanitizer after they dig in their noses, or scratch various private parts. So every time I shook someone's hand or touched someone's money, etc... I would be putting whatever germs and bacteria they had on their hands into my mouth with every nail bite. That realization seriously grossed me out and immediately made me sick to my stomach, but sadly it did not make me stop biting my nails, mostly because most of the time I had no idea that I was biting my fingernails until someone mentioned it or until I bit them so deep to cause pain or bleeding. The only thing this nasty realization was able to do for me was to cause me to wash my hands over and over again, excessively each day. I was told that my nail-biting was a nervous condition that was either related to stress, boredom, heredity, or all three. After so many years of trying to stop without success, I began to think nail-biting was a disease or mental block of some sort. For a period as a young teenager, I believed that maybe I was possessed by some demon and needed deliverance. It seems funny now as I'm writing this but I was serious about it back then.

Honestly, I was so tired, embarrassed, and fed up with this horrible habit that I no longer cared how nail-biting starts or what causes it, I just wanted to stop, period! Enough was enough! Due to the fact that you are reading this, I am assuming that you are fed up as well and all you just really want is to stop biting your nails. You can start getting excited because, by the time you're done reading this little book, you will know how to stop. I will keep it short, sweet, and to the point. The solution I discovered is embarrassingly simple, yet phenomenally effective. It just makes sense. It has worked in my life and in the lives of those who have followed my simple technique. It is these same people who have encouraged me to write this little book so that the whole world can have this solution in the palm of their hands. So let's get to it.

Victory

Chapter Three

THE SOLUTION

Every nail-biter I have asked agrees that the most damage to their fingernails is done without their conscious awareness or knowledge of the nail-biting. I am willing to bet that most of the time you do not even know you are biting your nails until you either hit a nerve by biting too deep, maybe you cause your fingers to bleed, or someone says to you, "Stop biting your nails." Whenever my best friend would see me biting my nails he would ask me if I wanted some salt with that. It was funny and embarrassing at the same time. Some of the remedies I tried worked for a short while, maybe a week or two at most, but eventually, everything failed. All except this one lifestyle change that I am going to tell you about right now. That is exactly what my solution is, a change in how you live every day regarding your nails.

This solution does not involve creams, gels, pills, hypnosis, etc... All you need is to be fed up, diligent, and determined to have success. There is no such thing as trying, only accomplishing or not. I am sure you have tried to avoid your nails or tried to keep your hands busy in an effort to stop nail biting, but to no avail. I know I did. I tried for many years to just mentally, physically, and in every other way possible to simply ignore my nails in an attempt to stop biting them. But like I have said before and I am sure you can attest to it, we mostly bite our nails naturally without even realizing we are doing it. So ignoring them was irrelevant to my success.

Then one day I thought to myself that if I cannot get myself to leave my nails alone, then maybe I should pay them way more attention than normal. I decided to constantly and continually look after my nails and by doing so, I believed it was naturally almost impossible to destroy something that I am constantly putting so much work into building up. To test my theory, I swallowed my pride and did something that I would have never done if I had not been truly fed up and disgusted with my habit. I went to the nail salon and got a manicure. This was very difficult for me for a couple of reasons. First, because I was embarrassed being that I was the only male in the nail shop, and secondly because I was humiliated and I almost walked out of the salon when the nail technician said, "Wow! Mister, you have to stop biting your nails, they look bad." If it was only that simple. In my anger and embarrassment, I wanted to give a smart reply like, "That's a great idea, I appreciate the revelation. Thank you for telling me." But I simply nodded my head. I was extremely embarrassed! But a few good things came from that experience.

The first benefit was that the little bit of nails I still had left on my fingers were filed and shaped into something a little more presentable. The best she could do with the mangled nubs I had left for her to work with. Also, the manicure as a whole felt wonderful, after the filing and cuticle removal, my hands were massaged from my fingertips to my wrist, and then my entire hand was dipped in warm wax which left my skin feeling wonderfully soft and smooth. At that moment I could then see why women would pay money for a manicure instead of doing it themselves.

The second benefit of this initial manicure was that in the end, my fingernails looked better than they had ever looked in my whole entire life, no exaggeration. Although to a person who has never bitten their nails, to them my nails would still look deformed.

The third benefit is that the manicure caused me to pay a great deal of positive attention to my nails. I felt more self-esteem, self-confidence, and self-assurance. I suffered intentional embarrassment to get my nails done and paid my hard-earned cash for that embarrassment but was repeatedly shocked and enamored with the new look and feel of my fingers.

Honestly, my fingernails were a far cry from nice looking but much better looking than the scarred and bloody nubs I normally had every day of my life before the manicure.

Last but definitely not least, that whole manicure experience and the days that followed it absolutely confirmed my idea or my theory. If I continually give my fingernails positive attention, then I cannot or I can hardly pay them negative attention like biting my fingernails.

I began to feel empowered as I started to believe in this idea or solution. Life seemed to confirm to me that I was on the right track.

The Solution

Likewise, you will begin to feel empowered as you start believing in this solution because it just makes sense. I went to the nail salon and got a manicure every week until my money became too scarce, but I had watched enough times to learn what she was doing. So I went to the beauty supply and bought the same tools so that I could take care of my own nails. Everything came to under $10.00. I could have gotten even cheaper items and paid less if I had chosen to do so.

You should always have a nail file handy along with fingernail clippers. Fingernail clippers with a metal fingernail file inside are ideal. You can keep it on a keychain so that you never have to put your hands in your mouth to fix a cracked, chipped, or jagged nail. It is also helpful for removing dead skin or rough cuticles around the nails - instead of using your teeth!

Using your tools constantly, and deliberately checking your nails for these imperfections will eliminate the normal habit of biting. Keep hands and fingers lotioned always. This will help prevent the urge to put them in your mouth and bite off the dead skin around the fingernails. The lotion's taste and smell will also alert you as soon as you put it in your mouth. Fingernails take a while to grow in and to begin to look normal, so be patient.

The Solution

If you have any oils or cuticle creams, clear nail polish for men, etc. Keep it in your pocket or purse always and apply it every time you can, every time you think about it, just do it. It does not matter if you just oiled your nails and cuticles an hour ago, do it again every time you think about it. I would set an alarm to go off every 30 mins at work so that I could do something positive to my nails, even if it was just applying cuticle oil. If I did not want to physically or if I could not physically do something to care for my nails, maybe because I was at work or driving, or maybe because I had just done something physically to my nails. I would simply visualize or imagine my nails long and attractive. I would imagine someone saying to me, "Wow William, your nails look great". I would imagine my children saying "Wow Dad how did you stop biting your nails after all these years." Trust me these things kept me from putting my fingers in my mouth.

Nail-biting was a way of life for me, not just the nail-biting but the comforting lifelong habit of placing my fingers in my mouth. It was completely subconscious. It happened normally without my conscious awareness. So the alarms broke up my routines and habits of how I normally lived with my nails. I used to apply clear nail polish and remove it every few days and reapply it. Again it was difficult to bite them at the same time as I was taking care of them.

Whatever you put the most on purpose energy into will prevail. nail-biting can be involuntary but nail care is intentional and nail care will grow stronger and become more natural as you continue.

Something else I implemented later in my nail growth journey after I was already having some success but I honestly felt like it took me to another level. I would every day as often as I thought of it. Look at my nails and say to myself out loud if I could or internally if I could not, that my hands and fingernails are aesthetically pleasing, that my nails are extremely attractive, strong, and healthy. There were times when I felt like an absolute liar, a fraud. At times it honestly was uncomfortable to say that especially after I had just finished biting them and they were bleeding, etc. Then I would remind myself of the verses of scripture that state, "speak those things that be not as though they were already", or "You shall have what you say" or verses like, "let the weak say I am strong, let the poor say I am rich" Then I did not feel like such a liar to myself. It worked because today all those things are completely true of my fingernails.

As a man, I had to deal with some funny looks as I applied the clear polish to my nails, but the growth and change in my nails were well worth it. Besides it was not nearly as embarrassing as the looks of disgust or sadness I would get after someone saw my bloody nubs. The taste of the polish would also help notify me of my fingers entering my mouth. You can use whatever chemicals or tricks you like to help your nails grow faster, or nothing at all. This Stop nail-biting solution works with or without it. But grandma's advice, nail growth oils or solutions, etc can only help you if you are using them to aid in your nail care. Remember it is the regular and on-purpose love you give to your nails that makes it difficult for you to harm your fingernails. Scripture says, "Sweet water and bitter water cannot come out of the same fountain". You will not be able to harm your nails and heal them at the same time.

I want to interject something else at this point. Another solution that has been found to help a lot of women has been to get acrylic nails placed over your own nails. This can allow your nails to grow and make it almost impossible for you to bite them while the acrylic nails are present. Some women I have spoken to have had no negative effects from acrylic nails, while others say that even though there is nail growth, it tends to leave their nails very weak and brittle, so they break off with the slightest use and are often very painful. Only through trial can you know how your nails will respond. It should also be noted that the majority of women whose

nails could successfully survive the acrylic nails,

stated that because their nail-biting habit was

not broken, they ended up biting their

fingernails off before they even realized they

had done it. A few Ladies mentioned that they

kept the acrylic nails on long enough to break

the nail-biting habit and it did work for them

long term. You can see if that works for you.

With that said, I believe you Ladies have a few

options:

1) You can continually (all your life) keep

the acrylic nails on.

2) Use acrylic nails to help your nail

growth start, then use the solution of

lifestyle change that I mention in this booklet to keep the nail growth you have acquired during the use of acrylic nails.

3) Use my solution by itself and immediately see a change in your habit without risking more damage to your nails. This solution truly worked for me immediately. If you fall or relapse into nail-biting, do not give up, do not beat yourself up, just get back to the plan and you will absolutely succeed. Believe me, I had to get back up again and again, but if you do not give up, it will work. I promise!

The results were so immediate, the change in my behavior as well as my fingernail growth was so clearly noticeable that whenever I did fall back into the habit of biting my nails, it was easy to get back on the plan. You will not have to do this forever, just long enough to break that horrible habit. Again you simply replace the subconscious nail-biting habit with a conscious habit of nail care. Please believe it will get much easier, and become much more natural to not bite your nails. After some time, biting your nails will seem almost foreign to you. I guarantee it!! Just be diligent and consistent.

Just to reiterate the solution: I want you to pay an extreme amount of positive attention to caring for your nails, continually do good and soothing things to your hands and fingers, look after them, always say positive things about your fingernails, clean them and polish them. While you are sitting at home in front of the television or computer, gently and slowly massage a soothing oil into each fingernail individually. It feels amazing, you will feel relaxed, and you will be doing positive things to your nails and caring for yourself. You cannot bite them and gently massage oil into them at the same time. These new good behaviors will over time replace the negative self-destructive behaviors we hold towards our fingernails. Try it and see for yourself.

The Solution

Men can apply clear nail polish to their nails if they want. I have used clear polish on my nails many times during this process. As a matter of fact, when I got my manicures, clear polish was always applied to my fingernails. File them, buff them, lotion them and never use your teeth to do any of this. It is written, "God's way is so simple a fool can not err." Many times simple solutions are the best and most lasting solutions. Please do not let the simplicity of this solution hinder you from believing in it. You can get victory in this area of your life, right now. This solution works. It is simple, immediately effective, it will change your bad habit and You can do it today!

Chapter Four

YOUR TOOLS

Your nails are always growing, you do not truly need things to cause your fingernails to grow, we simply need to curb the actions that hinder our natural nail growth. We should always have these tools at hand or easily accessible at all times. Buy them small if you wish. I bought them small so that they could easily fit in my pocket.

FINGERNAIL FILE: Use this to always keep your nails filed down and neat. This will eliminate the need to try to fix jagged or rough nails with your teeth.

FINGERNAIL CLIPPER: Use this to remove chipped nails or dead skin from around fingernails.

CUTICLE REMOVER: This can be very sharp, so please be very careful. Use this to remove cuticles from nails. I believe and many people I have asked agree that raggedy cuticles and dead skin around fingernails are one of the greatest temptations to consciously or on purpose put our fingers in our mouths. The rationale is that you're not biting your nails, just removing unsightly dead skin or ragged cuticles, but this always, always leads to nail-biting. I want to mention that many people as well as the Mayo Clinic have stated that you should not cut off your cuticles even at the nail shop because it is bad for your nail growth. I am not certain of the validity of that statement, you should do your own research and decide for yourself but I can attest to how easy it is to dig too deep into my cuticles with those very sharp cuticle removers so, please be very careful or just allow the professionals to do them for you if you choose to have your cuticles removed.

CUTICLE OIL: Cuticle oil is an oil used to hydrate and moisturize the nail bed. It is a moisturizing product typically derived from vegetable oils and greatly improves the health and longevity of your nails and cuticles. It is a nourishing product that can positively affect circulation and nail growth. Our hands are continuously exposed; cuticle oil is a perfect solution for when our fingernails begin to look cracked, chapped, or dry. Cuticle oil helps to strengthen and thicken the nails. It helps rejuvenate our nails and it acts as an extra barrier to protect your nail polish. Cuticle oil is a gentle product that is safe for people with sensitive skin. Therefore, not only should its application be free of irritation, but it also will likely heal the damage that may have accumulated around or on your fingernails, cuticles, and surrounding skin.

POCKET SIZE HAND LOTION: Keeping fingers lotioned can help you keep fingers out of your mouth by providing a smell and taste that can alert you to unconscious biting and can keep your fingers looking smooth. Excessively dry fingers seem to show a lot of tempting dead or dry skin for you to want to quickly remove with your teeth. Anything else that you might want to use that will cause you to take better care of your nails or hands is a plus. Remember you want to pay a lot of positive attention to your hands; you want to care for them continually. This type of care or attention to your hands and nails will eliminate the urge to bite them,

consciously or unconsciously.

Chapter Five

NAIL CARE

I wanted to give you more information than just my opinion or my experience from decades of nail-biting so this is from the Mayo Clinic. Your fingernails — composed of laminated layers of a protein called keratin — grow from the area at the base of the nail under your cuticle. Healthy fingernails are smooth, without pits or grooves. They're uniform in color and consistency and free of spots or discoloration.

Sometimes fingernails develop harmless vertical ridges that run from the cuticle to the tip of the nail. Vertical ridges tend to become more prominent with age. Fingernails can also develop white lines or spots due to injury, but these eventually grow out with the nail.

Not all nail conditions are normal, however. Consult your doctor or dermatologist if you notice:

- Changes in nail color, such as discoloration of the entire nail or a dark streak under the nail
- Changes in nail shape, such as curled nails
- Thinning or thickening of the nails

- Separation of the nail from the surrounding skin

- Bleeding around the nails

- Swelling or pain around the nails

- Failure of nails to grow out

Fingernail care: Do's

To keep your fingernails looking their best:

- **Keep fingernails dry and clean.** This prevents bacteria from growing under your fingernails. Repeated or prolonged contact with water can contribute to split fingernails. Wear cotton-lined rubber gloves when washing dishes, cleaning, or using harsh chemicals.

- **Practice good nail hygiene.** Use sharp manicure scissors or clippers. Trim your nails straight across, then round the tips in a gentle curve.

- **Use moisturizer.** When you use hand lotion, rub the lotion into your fingernails and cuticles, too.

- **Apply a protective layer.** Applying a nail hardener might help strengthen nails.

- **Ask your doctor about biotin.** Some research suggests that the nutritional supplement biotin might help strengthen weak or brittle fingernails.

Fingernail care: Don'ts

To prevent nail damage, do not:

- **Bite your fingernails or pick at your cuticles.** These habits can damage the nail bed. Even a minor cut alongside your fingernail can allow bacteria or fungi to enter and cause an infection.

- **Pull off hangnails.** You might rip live tissue along with the hangnail. Instead, carefully clip off hangnails.

- **Use harsh nail care products.** Limit your use of nail polish remover.

When using nail polish remover, opt for an acetone-free formula.

- **Ignore problems.** If you have a nail problem that doesn't seem to go away on its own or is associated with other signs and symptoms, consult your doctor or dermatologist for an evaluation.

A note about manicures and pedicures

If you rely on manicures or pedicures for healthy-looking nails, keep a few things in mind. Stick to salons that display a current state license, and work only with technicians also licensed by the state board. do not have your cuticles removed — they act to seal the skin to the nail plate, so removal can lead to nail infection. Also, make sure your nail technician properly sterilizes all tools used during your procedure to prevent the spread of infection.

You might also ask how the foot baths are cleaned. Ideally, a bleach solution is used between clients and the filters are cleaned regularly.

It is easy to neglect your nails — but taking some basic steps can keep your fingernails healthy and strong.

Freedom

Chapter Six

WHY DO WE BITE OUR NAILS?

An article on Healthline.com Medically reviewed by Cynthia Cobb, DNP, APRN, WHNP-BC, FAANP — Written by Ann Pietrangelo on August 26, 2020, states that. Many people bite their nails at some point, especially as children. It is a type of body-focused repetitive behavior that goes by the clinical name of onychophagia. There's a spectrum of nail-biting. It can range from an occasional benign behavior to a deeply ingrained self-mutilative behavior. Many people who begin biting their nails as children eventually outgrow the habit. For others, it becomes a lifelong habit that can be extremely difficult to quit. Let's take a closer look at why people bite their nails.

Psychology of nail-biting

About half of all kids and teens bite their nails. Many of us do not grow out of it, either. If you're an adult who bites your nails, you may have done it when you were younger and just never stopped. Scientists are not sure if nail-biting is genetic, but kids whose parents bite their nails are more likely to bite their nails, as well. Studies show this happens even if the parents stop doing it before their child is born. Sometimes, nail biting can be a sign of emotional or mental stress. It tends to show up in people who are nervous, anxious, or feeling down. It is a way to cope with these feelings. You may also find yourself doing it when you're bored, hungry or feeling insecure. Most nail-biting is automatic -- you do it without thinking or even realizing it. nail-biting typically begins in childhood and may accelerate during adolescence. It is not always clear why someone develops this particular habit, but once it starts, it can be difficult to manage.

Impatience, frustration, boredom

Once nail-biting becomes a habit, it can become your go-to behavior when you're waiting around, frustrated, or just plain bored. it is something you do to keep yourself occupied.

Concentration

Sometimes, it is just an absentminded tendency rather than a conscious choice during moments of intense concentration. You might not be aware that you're biting your nails while trying to work out a problem.

Stress, anxiety

Biting your nails can be a nervous habit, possibly an effort to find temporary relief from stress and anxiety.

Emotional or psychological problems

nail-biting can be associated with mental health

conditions, such as:

- attention deficit hyperactivity disorder (ADHD)
- major depressive disorder (MDD)
- obsessive-compulsive disorder (OCD)
- oppositional defiant disorder
- separation anxiety disorder
- Tourette syndrome

Not everyone with these disorders bites their nails. By the same token, biting your nails doesn't mean you have a psychological disorder.

Strength

Chapter Seven

SIDE EFFECTS AND RISKS

Nail-biting can include biting the nail, the cuticle, and the tissue around the nail. Most nail biters do not develop long-term damage, but it can happen.

Beyond soreness of the nails and surrounding skin, side effects can include:

- abnormal-looking nails
- fungal infections of the nail plate and surrounding skin

- illness due to passing bacteria and viruses from your fingers to your face and mouth

- harm to teeth such as chipping, misalignment, and dental resorption

- temporomandibular joint pain and dysfunction

In addition, habits like swallowing bitten-off nails can increase the risk of stomach and intestinal infections.

nail-biting is a repetitive behavior that ranges from mild to severe. It usually starts in childhood. While some people outgrow it, it can become a lifelong habit. Most of the time, nail biting is a harmless cosmetic problem that doesn't require medical care. But severe nail-biting can lead to infection, dental problems, and other issues that need to be treated. There are several strategies that can help you stop biting your nails. Figuring out the cause is helpful, though it is not always clear. Figuring out the cause helped me as well as using different strategies but only the change of lifestyle practice I mentioned in this book was able to change my life and habit on a lasting basis in regards to my nail-biting and I am certain it will work for you as well. Like the scriptures say, "Oh Taste and See". In other words, try it for yourself. What have you got to lose other than this horrible, self-destructive habit?

Healing

Chapter Eight

THE LIFE LESSONS

From overcoming years of nail-biting I have learned a few things. I applied this solution to other areas of my life and received the same kind of success. I have come to believe this solution is based on some natural mental and spiritual truths that can aid us in everyday living, and overcoming issues, fears, and phobias in our lives. Let's get into it. Scripture says that all things work together for our good. Because of the many decades of nail-biting and struggling to stop it, I discovered a bunch of other revelations about life from this process that I would like to share with you.

Life Lesson Number One:

"You ain't gone, never be nothing in life, that's why you bite your nails!" I realize that this is an improper sentence but it is word for word what my Grandmother said to me when I was 13 years old. Growing up my brother and I rarely saw our mother's parents. I kinda felt like my mother was hindering us from going to visit with our grandparents so the summer after I turned 13, feeling like a full teenager now. I asked my mother If I could walk maybe 5 or 6 miles to my Grandparents' house and she said yes I could. Shortly after walking in the door at my grandparents, feeling accomplished, mature and excited to see my family. My Grandmother sitting on the sofa asked me what I had been up to. I said, just going to school, in the youth choir, and that I had a role in the church play coming up.

My grandmother's instant response, interrupting me was, "You ain't gone, never be nothing in life, that's why you bite your nails!" I froze, I did not know how to respond. I waited to see if she was joking with me but she just stared directly at me from behind her eyeglasses waiting for my response. I tried to figure out what I had said or done to make her upset with me but I was baffled. At that moment I realized possibly why my Mom had kept us at a distance from her Mom and Dad or maybe my Grandparents simply did not want us to come over. Nonetheless, I never tried to visit again after that encounter. But my grandmother's words about me haunted me my entire life.

I dealt with many issues growing up. I was constantly bullied, I had an abusive stepdad and I wrestled continually with anxiety and depression leading to suicidal thoughts often. On top of that, I was a very serious church boy. Growing up engulfed in religion we were taught that we had to humble ourselves, that we were sinners who God was gonna send to hell to burn for eternity if Jesus had not died for our sins. Meaning we were still dirty rotten sinners but covered by the blood of Jesus. We were taught that our righteousness is as filthy rags, that our flesh was corrupted and our enemy and it was our constant job while in this body to crucify our flesh with its affections and lusts. Wow! Looking back on it now, no wonder I had such an amazingly low opinion of myself. My self-talk was continually self-deprecating in an attempt to keep myself humble. Believing it made me closer to God. As if I really needed any help feeling more inadequate in life. Please allow me to make it clear that not all churches teach this way, many of them do not but I attended a few growing up that did. I know that their intentions were good and pure but damaging nonetheless. The point I am making with this short version of this time period in my life is how life itself handed me low value for myself and because of my religious beliefs, I not only accepted them, I welcomed those thoughts about myself. I believed they helped me to be more humble which equated in my mind to being more Godly. But as I matured into manhood. I began to realize how those negative thoughts I embraced about myself and continually said about myself, negatively affected every area of my life. Like how I raised my children, how I loved my wife, how I treated my neighbor, how

I handled my job, and even how I loved God. Insecurities ran my life, they were what my character and personality were based on or rooted in.

The way I was able to escape that ingrained system of mental self-destruction was the exact same technique I used to stop biting my fingernails. Let me explain. Because of all these things not only were my actual words about myself always negative, but my inner dialogue and even my feelings about myself were self-deprecating. So just as I did my fingernails, I began to put conscious effort into loving myself with positive words of affirmation. Over and over again, day and night, I would constantly say good things about myself, loving things, encouraging things, and kind things about myself. Honestly, It felt so odd at first, it was a struggle. I felt like an absolute liar and a fraud.

But I pressed forward and continued. Like the bible says, "speak those things that are not as though they were", also "let the weak say I am strong and Let the poor say I am rich". I would say things like, "I am intelligent, I am wonderful, I love and value myself, I am talented, I am handsome, I am wise, I am a great father, I am Loving and Kind to everyone", etc. In all honesty, the first time I ever uttered the words to myself that I loved myself, I was nearly half a century old. Over time it became easier and easier till one day I began to believe these positive and encouraging things about myself. Over time this positive self-talk began to outshine the decades of negative self-talk and negative beliefs about myself. I was becoming a different person, a much better person, and even my family members noticed. It was an absolutely life-changing experience! Again, I used the exact same technique I mention in this book.

Life Lesson Number Two:

In my teenage years thru my early 30s, I would occasionally, maybe every couple of months have a horrible dream that I was suffocating. The Dreams were so intense that each time I would wake up gasping for breath, each time feeling like I had almost died. The fear I felt would stay with me throughout most of my day. In my 20's being desperate for help I even embarrassed myself by telling a bunch of ministers at church but they just looked at me like they felt sorry for me and said they would keep me in prayer. I just tried to ignore it, to not think about it until it would happen again.

In my 30s realizing that these horrifying dreams were not ever gonna stop, I began analyzing the dreams and what could be causing them. Then I learned that when I was a baby my father would throw covers over my face when I would cry so he did not have to hear me. Which made sense because that explained why I could not sleep unless I had a blanket or pillow on my head. But an odd thing happened, the more understanding I received as to why I might be having the nightmares only seemed to cause them to happen more often. The nightmares grew worse and more often. I was terrified, now even when I was not having the dream just the thought that I might have one the next time I went to bed would horrify me. Eventually, that fear morphed into all-out panic attacks in the middle of the day. Anything that covered my nose or hindered my breathing in the slightest caused immediate hyperventilating till I could calm myself down.

I tried all kinds of prayer and counseling for years but nothing seemed to work until I remembered how I stopped biting my nails. I rationalized that pain is not our enemy, it is our friend, it is trying to protect us but because it hurts us we tend to view pain as an adversary or enemy. But if it was not for pain how many times would I have burned my hand off on a stove while not paying attention etc? So, I immediately began to start thanking my mind for my fears. I began saying to myself I appreciate my mind and imagination for trying to protect me because that is all fear really is although my fears had taken over my life and were haunting me in my dreams and panic attacks during the day. I had to believe that beneath all that was my mind trying to protect me and that because of the many years of despising those dreams and fears I only made them worse so I started to change my viewpoint about them.

It felt very odd for a while but I was desperate for freedom, just like I was from nail-biting so I had to try it and long story short, little by little over time the dreams completely vanished, and the panic attracts became manageable fears to eventually nonexistent fears. Fear and Love cannot live together. One has to go. Even the bible says that "Perfect Love casts out Fear." Just as nail-biting and nail-loving cannot live together one has to go. If I tell you not to think about your phone, no matter how many times I say it, you will automatically think about your phone, honestly the more I tell you not to, the more you will. It seems to be human nature, so the more I tried to push those fears away the stronger and more frequent they became but as soon as I allowed them to be and simply began embracing them they immediately began to have less and less hold on my life. I thought about those fears on purpose but in positive ways and I freed myself from that fear entirely. In Buddhism, they believe that since our mind creates everything, no external cause is really creating any pain for us. It is only the illusion within our mind that creates the pain we feel. The external cause is what draws our attention to the pain that already exists. Let that marinate.

Life Lesson Number Three:

I felt like I kept saying the wrong things at the wrong time and I would constantly beat myself up about it. I continued to do that even after becoming a grandfather which was even more upsetting because I assumed that I would get wiser with age and no longer make that error but the more I disliked it and beat myself up about it the more I did it until one day I again remembered my nail-biting lesson and began saying to myself on purpose that "I always say the right thing, at the right time, in the right way" and whenever I did mess up I did not beat myself up, I would just act like I did say the right thing at the right time in the right way. Till I hardly ever made that mistake again.

Scripture states that sweet water and bitter water cannot come from the same fountain. We can beat ourselves up or love ourselves but we cannot do both at the same time. One response increases what we do not like about ourselves and the other changes us. It is up to us. In a book by Don Miguel Ruiz titled, "The Four Agreements" he mentions that people are experiencing life as the result of their own reflection in a mirror. Two people walking in the street on a rainy day, and a bus passes by too close to the curb soaking them both. Chances are their reactions will be very different. This is because of our internal issues and subjective perceptions of the world. One of them may be annoyed but decides to laugh at it, while the other one is still screaming and swearing at the bus driver. The first one will recover from this in the next 5 minutes and the second one will still be mad the next day. Instead of continually struggling against things we do not want we should simply embrace those things and allow them to dissipate. I think a lot of times we take a shovel and attempt to shovel the darkness from our lives. Maybe shoveling the darkness is an enormous amount of useless struggle as well as a waste of time. I have found that the best way to get rid of the darkness in my life is to simply turn on the lights. My stop nail-biting theory simply helps us to turn on the lights. Try it for yourself.

Life Lesson Number Four:

I even tried this with an external situation. But it began as an internal trial. I felt like I had been a bad father. I was married and a stepdad at 19. Within the next several years we had three more children. I was very immature and extremely unprepared to be either married or a father. I made many, many mistakes. So I continually beat myself up for decades about how I messed up as a father. Again I remembered the lesson I learned from my stop-nail-biting experience. I wanted to heal more things about myself so I began saying I am a great father and I did the best I could with what I had. All the mistakes I made while raising my kids will work out for their good, etc. I began feeling a lot better internally, I began forgiving myself and it honestly made me a better father and grandfather. The external proof was not just how I felt about myself but my grown children out of nowhere began to tell me how good of a dad I was raising them and how awesome of a dad I was now. WOW!

This is the same method I applied to stop biting my nails. Swiss psychologist Carl Jung stated that "What you resist not only persists but will grow in size." When we feel suffering, sadness, or any kind of emotional pain, our instinct is to resist it. In some ways, it feels right to resist what hurts and frightens us. It is simply not in our human nature to embrace suffering or pain. But pain is not the cause of the problem, it is usually only the symptom of the true issue. Is it possible that when we resist things we are pulling them closer to us? Whatever we resist, persists.

Life Lesson Number Five:

I had gained a bunch of weight. My son walked up to me and said, "Dad, you look like you are pregnant." I was so embarrassed. So I began my weight loss journey. It was a struggle. I would do well for a moment then crash and burn, spectacularly. Again, I would be doing good at losing weight and working out then I would again, pig out and fail miserably. But because I would not give up, because I continued to eat better and go to the gym. I felt like my body was fighting against me but really it was only trying to give me what I wanted. I had conditioned my body and brain to want honey buns, Twinkies, ice cream, gummy bears, big macs, fried chicken, Chinese food, pork ribs, etc...

These are the things I loved and my body was used to getting them whenever I wanted them so when I began telling my body and brain No, they began to struggle with me. Not because they were my adversaries but simply because I had conditioned myself to continually enjoy these things often. But I believe our bodies are designed to work for us, not against us. My body was simply behaving as I had trained it to behave. Consider a very healthy eater. They crave their salads, fruits, water, smoothies, etc, and if they go to eat at a fast-food restaurant, watch their bodies rebel against it. They are likely to get very sick, have a bad headache or at the least an upset stomach, and feel completely drained physically as their body struggles to digest this foreign substance called fast food. Our bodies are not our enemies, we do not need to struggle against them. Is it possible that our bodies are designed to assist us in life and we simply need to train them to do what we desire? Same thing when I began working out. It was such a chore, I had to use all my willpower and focus to ensure that I would go get my workout in. I would fail and not go, then I would begin going back again but eventually, because I was consistent in going to the gym over time it became fun. My body and my mind began looking forward to it. Over time it would get better, and it would get easier. I began to fall in love with working out, with the idea of eating healthy. I began looking forward to my salads, fruit, etc. I started to feel lighter and more energetic.

Now in my 50's I honestly feel like my life is lacking if I am not in the gym at least 5 days a week. I rarely miss a day, even while traveling. I absolutely love what I used to despise. I experience pleasure mentally, spiritually, and physically not only after my workouts but during. I cut my phone on silent while I am working out. It has become a time of self-love and peace. I get revelations, insights, and great ideas while I am working out. As a matter of fact, the idea of how to arrange this book occurred to me during leg day.

It works the same way as we are healing our nails. We are putting our energy and focus on loving our nails in action, words, and vision. We may fall and mess up and bite our nails. Following this solution, we may have nail growth and be excited then something makes us nervous and we destroy our nails all over again. We have to remind ourselves to not get upset with ourselves, and not to give up on ourselves. Like the scripture says, "In due season we will reap if we faint not." Do Not faint, YOU GOT THIS!!

Life Lesson Number Six:

I grew up in church and grew up extremely religious with a strong fear of going to hell if I did not keep all of God's Holy commandments. I struggled for many, many years to keep what I believed were God's commandments and I suffered so many failures. I would have periods of strength where I felt like an absolute angel and then periods where I felt possessed by the devil. Remember what Swiss psychologist Carl Jung stated, that, What you resist persists. Seemed the more I struggled to keep the commandments the more I broke them. But at some point, I decided to focus on the greatest commandment that Jesus gave to love thy neighbor as myself, and just like magic, it became much easier to not break the commandments. I was no longer focused on what I did not want to do and instead, I began focusing on what I did want to do.

It is easy to not kill someone you love, to not steal from someone you are loving, to not lie to someone you are loving, etc. Remember sweet water and bitter water cannot come out of the same fountain. You will only have one or the other. This also is the exact same scenario I used to stop biting my fingernails. Take time to care for your nails, love on them, massage them, whisper sweet nothing to your fingernails, and watch them bloom and grow strong. What have you got to lose by trying? It worked for me, my

family, and my friends and it will work for you.

Chapter Nine

<u>WORDS OF ENCOURAGEMENT</u>

I want you to understand that the diligence that you are putting towards the care of your fingernails, the going out of your way, all the reminding yourself to care for your nails, setting timers, visualizing, etc is only temporary. These things are tools that are here only to help you break the bad habit that has become a part of your life, biting your nails. After a while, you will not have to do any of these things anymore.

If you follow the simple instructions in this book you will soon realize that you no longer have to take care of your fingernails every day. The bad habit will break, and you will soon have another lifestyle in regard to your fingernails. You will become used to not putting your fingers in your mouth. It does not really take that long at all, just some consistency and diligence. It is very likely that I had been biting my fingernails to the point of bleeding for a much longer period than the majority of my readers have been alive, so if I can beat this horrible habit, so can you.

You got this! You may mess up, and you may bite your nails during this process, but Never be upset with yourself. Never get sad or disappointed with yourself. It does not mean the process is not working. It is absolutely working. I did the same things repeatedly. But consistency and patience is the key! You got this!

You will look up and soon it will feel foreign for you to put your fingers in your mouth. It will seem odd and out of place for you to bite your nails. Watch and see!

You will notice your fingernails looking healthy, strong, and aesthetically pleasing to yourself as well as everyone else.

For those of us who have been biting our nails for thirty, forty, and 50 years, this solution can be totally life-changing because, after that many years of nail-biting and not being able to stop we would naturally begin to believe we could never and would never be able to stop and bloody, painful, unattractive nubs are a way of life for us for our entire life. But if you intentionally love on your nails, you cannot mistreat them. You cannot destroy them and love them at the same time. It sounds too simple to be true but it is absolutely true and it will work for you.

I hope this little book was everything I promised it to be. As I stated in the introduction. Within the pages of this little book, there is a simple yet phenomenally effective solution that will show you how to End fingernail-biting forever. No gimmicks, no tricks, no creams or chemicals. Just a proven way of ending the horrible habit of nail-biting. I gave you simple everyday actions that will immediately change your nail-biting behavior forever. Plus I tried to make this book short, sweet, and to the point.

You can STOP Today!

Thanks for reading and please share this book with other nail-biters you know!

Great Success to You in all areas of Life!

Sincerely,

W. E. Smith